● Name _____

Wrapping a prese

Colour the pictures. Cut them out and make a story.

ESSENTIALS FOR ENGLISH: Story sequencing

● Name _____

My lunch box

Colour the pictures. Cut them out and make a story.

● ESSENTIALS FOR ENGLISH: Story sequencing   6

● Name _____

Going swimming

Colour the pictures. Cut them out and make a story.

● ESSENTIALS FOR ENGLISH: Story sequencing

- **Name** _____

Feeding the cat

Colour the pictures. Cut them out and make a story.

ESSENTIALS FOR ENGLISH: Story sequencing

- Name _____

Humpty Dumpty

Colour the pictures. Cut them out.
Put them in order and make the rhyme.

Humpty Dumpty had a great fall.

Couldn't put Humpty together again.

Humpty Dumpty sat on the wall.

All the king's horses and all the king's men

- ESSENTIALS FOR ENGLISH: Story sequencing

Jack and Jill

Colour the pictures. Cut them out.
Put them in order and make the rhyme.

To fetch a pail of water.

Jack fell down and broke his crown

Jack and Jill went up the hill

And Jill came tumbling after.

Rags and the cat

1 Rags looked up.

2 He saw a cat.

3 'What shall I do?' said Rags.

"What shall I do?"

What happens next?

4

4

Copy the sentences to make the story.
Choose the ending you like best.
Make up the last sentence yourself.

1 _____

2 _____

3 _____

4 _____

Name _____

I want some sweets

| 1 | 2 | 3 |

'I want some sweets!'

'I want some sweets!'

'I want some sweets!'

What happens next?

| 4 | 4 |

Copy the sentences to make the story.
Choose the ending you like best.
Make up the last sentence yourself.

1 _____

2 _____

3 _____

4 _____

ESSENTIALS FOR ENGLISH: Story sequencing

Name _____

Mother hen

1	2	3
A hen sits on her eggs.	An egg begins to crack.	CRACK!

What happens next?

4	4

Copy the sentences to make the story.
Choose the ending you like best.
Make up the last sentence yourself.

1 _____
2 _____
3 _____
4 _____

ESSENTIALS FOR ENGLISH: Story sequencing

Name _____

Camping

Read the sentences and cut them out.
Put them in order, then stick them into your book.

They woke up.
They were very wet.

The children put up a tent in the garden.

They had supper.
They were having a lovely time.

'Can we sleep in the tent tonight?' they asked.
'Yes,' said Mum.

They ran into the house.
Mum made them hot drinks.

In the night it started to rain.
It rained and rained.

ESSENTIALS FOR ENGLISH: Story sequencing

The seasons

Read the sentences below. Cut them out.
Match the sentences to the pictures.

```
In summer the sun feels hot.
There is more daylight.
We can play outside.
```

```
In winter it gets dark early.
The weather is cold.
We need to keep warm.
```

```
In spring flowers and trees
start to grow.
It begins to get warmer.
```

```
In autumn, leaves fall from
the trees.
It begins to get colder.
```

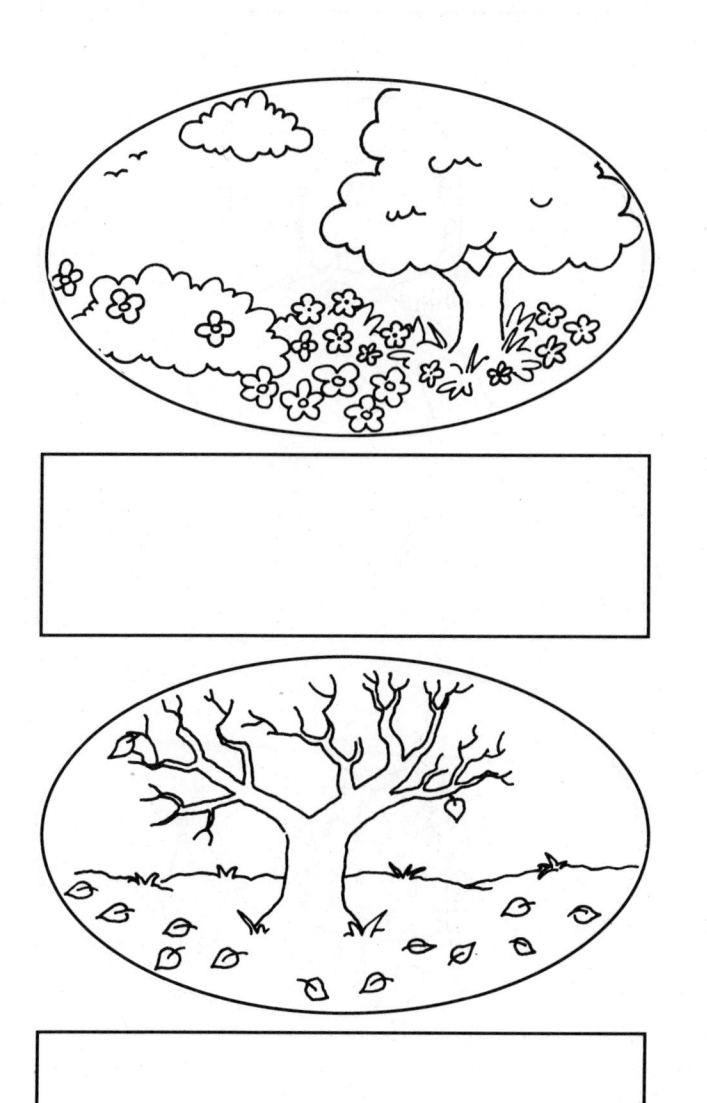

ESSENTIALS FOR ENGLISH: Story sequencing

21

Name _____

Growing up

Read the sentences below. Cut them out.
Match the sentences to the pictures.

I move slowly and my hair is going grey. I enjoy seeing my grandchildren.

I cannot walk or talk yet.
I drink a lot of milk.
I cry when I am hungry.

I can run and jump and I talk a lot. I can feed myself. I like playing with my friends.

Now I am grown up I can go to work.
I can drive a car.

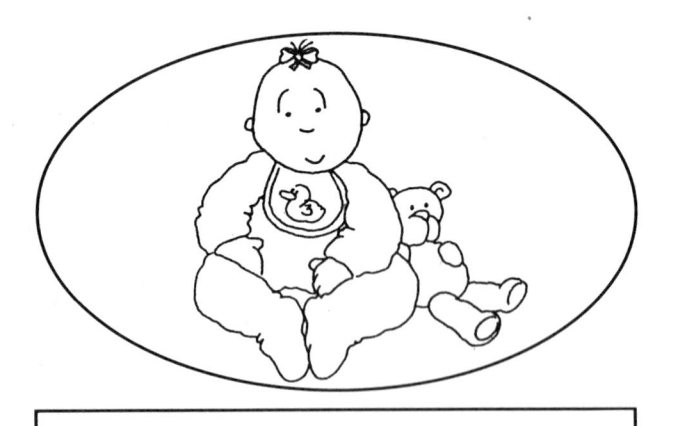

ESSENTIALS FOR ENGLISH: Story sequencing   22

● Name _____

Recycling paper

Read the sentences below. Cut them out.
Match the sentences to the pictures.

✂------------------------------
We take the bundles to the		We can use the paper again
lorry. The lorry takes the		to write our letters.
paper to the factory.		
-------------------------------   ------------------------------

| We save our newspapers. | | At the factory the paper is |
| We tie them into bundles. | | recycled. |
-------------------------------   ------------------------------

ESSENTIALS FOR ENGLISH: Story sequencing   23

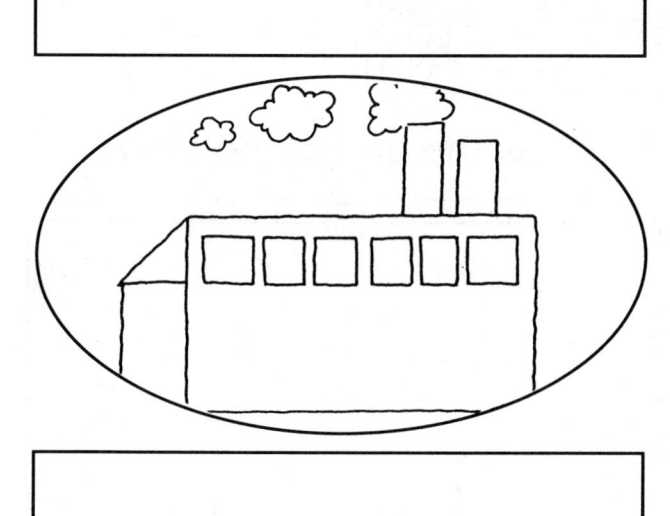

• Name _____

The hare and the tortoise

The ending of the story is missing. Can you finish it?

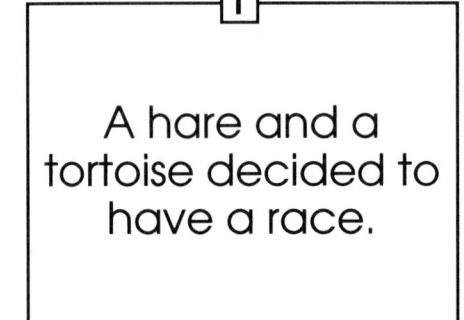

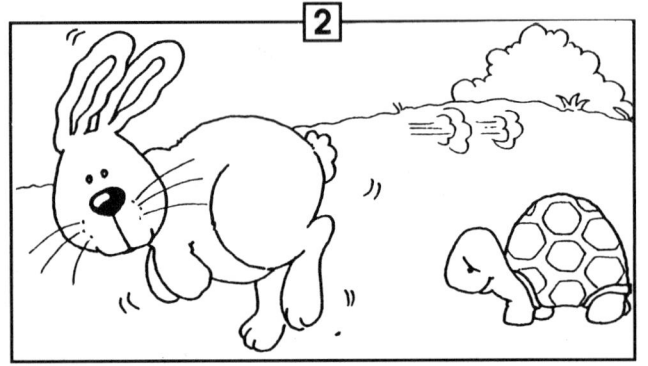

1
A hare and a tortoise decided to have a race.

2	3
	The hare had a rest. He sat down under the tree and fell fast asleep.

4

Write what happens.   Draw the end of the story.

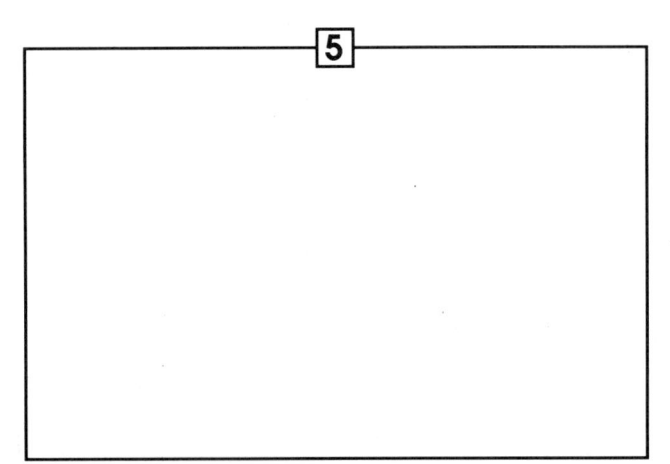

5	6

● ESSENTIALS FOR ENGLISH: Story sequencing   24

- Name _____

The lion and the mouse

The ending of the story is missing. Can you finish it?

1

2

'I am the strongest animal in the jungle!' said the lion.

3

4

'I can help you,' said the mouse.
'You are too small to help me,' said the lion.

Draw the end of the story.   Write what happens.

5

6

Cinderella

The ending of the story is missing. Can you finish it?

1

2
Cinderella couldn't go
to the ball.
The ugly sisters went
without her.
Cinderella cried.

3

4
Cinderella danced with
the prince at the ball.
She was very happy, but
she had to leave at
midnight.

Draw the end of the story.   Write what happens.

5

6

ESSENTIALS FOR ENGLISH: Story sequencing

26

● Name _____

Jack and the beanstalk

The ending of the story is missing. Can you finish it?

1

2
The next morning Jack
saw a beanstalk growing
into the sky.
He climbed and climbed
to the very top.

3

4
Jack waited until the
giant was asleep.
He took the hen and
ran off and climbed down
the beanstalk.

Draw the end of the story.　　　　Write what happens.

5　　　　**6**

● ESSENTIALS FOR ENGLISH: Story sequencing

● Name _____

Rocky the robot and the spaceship

Cut out the sentences. Put them in order to tell the story.

1. Rocky wanted to go to the moon.

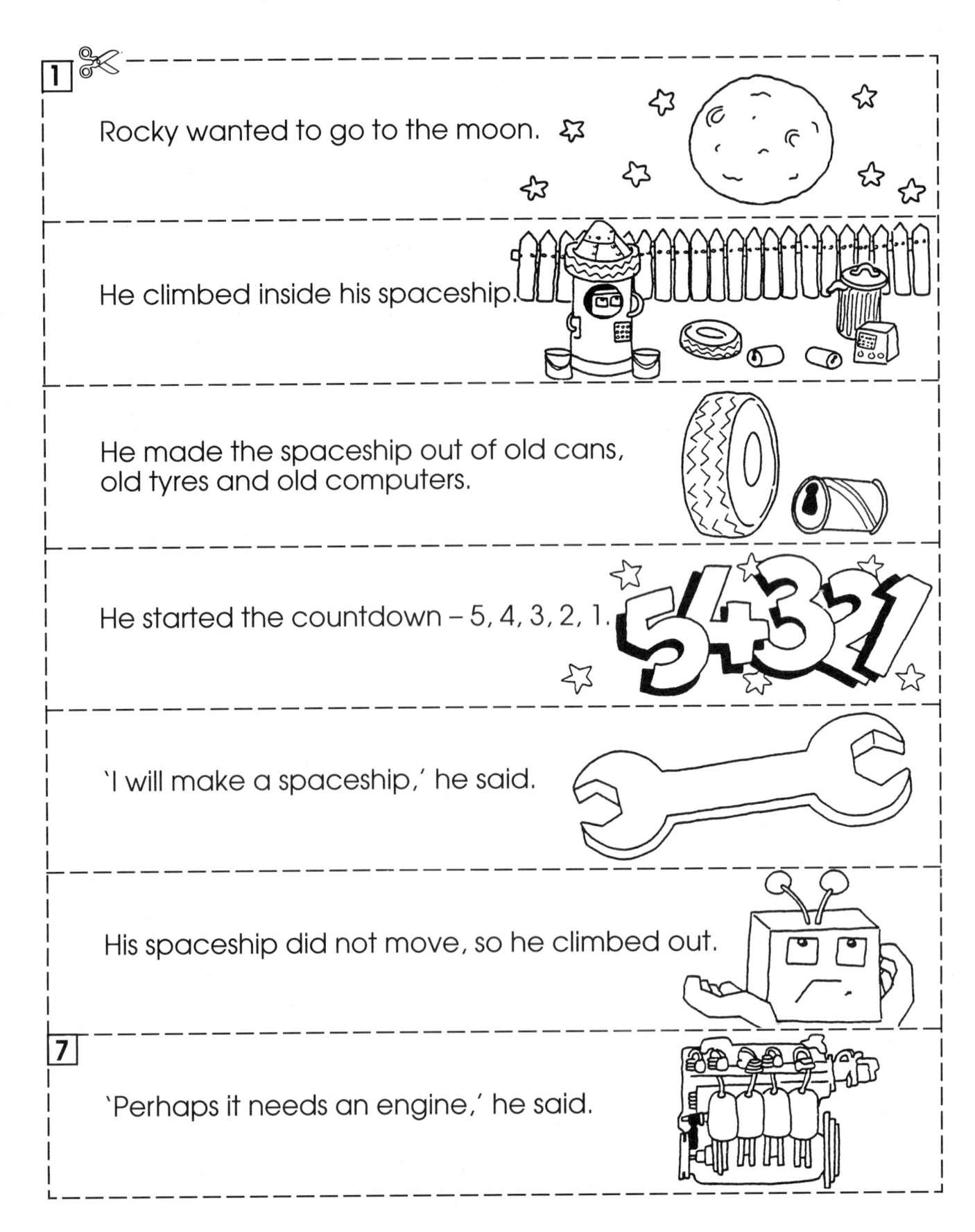

He climbed inside his spaceship.

He made the spaceship out of old cans, old tyres and old computers.

He started the countdown – 5, 4, 3, 2, 1.

'I will make a spaceship,' he said.

His spaceship did not move, so he climbed out.

7. 'Perhaps it needs an engine,' he said.

● ESSENTIALS FOR ENGLISH: Story sequencing

● Name _____

Rocky the robot and the supermarket

Cut out the sentences. Put them in order to tell the story.

1.
Rocky looked in his kitchen.
There was no food left.

He saw the trolleys by the door.
He took one and pushed it into the shop.

Rocky wanted to ride like that so he got into his trolley.

Rocky saw a little boy sitting in a trolley.

His trolley rolled into a pile of tins.
The tins fell into his trolley.

'I must go shopping,' said Rocky.
So he went to the supermarket.

7.
'That's lucky,' said Rocky.
'I wanted to buy lots of beans.'

● ESSENTIALS FOR ENGLISH: Story sequencing

29

Name _____

The fox and the crow

Colour the pictures. Cut out the paragraphs.
Put them in order to tell the story.

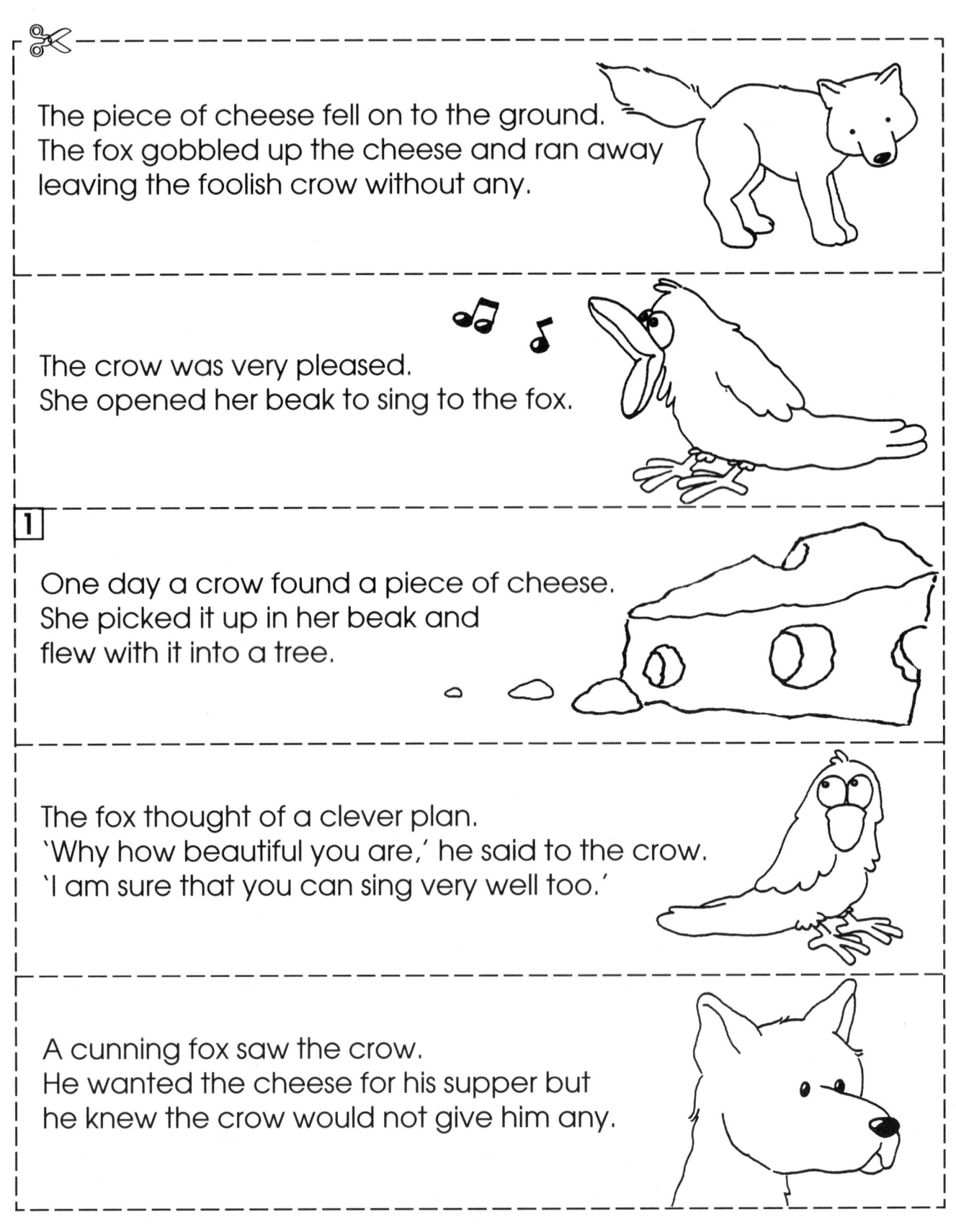

The piece of cheese fell on to the ground.
The fox gobbled up the cheese and ran away
leaving the foolish crow without any.

The crow was very pleased.
She opened her beak to sing to the fox.

---

[1]

One day a crow found a piece of cheese.
She picked it up in her beak and
flew with it into a tree.

The fox thought of a clever plan.
'Why how beautiful you are,' he said to the crow.
'I am sure that you can sing very well too.'

A cunning fox saw the crow.
He wanted the cheese for his supper but
he knew the crow would not give him any.

ESSENTIALS FOR ENGLISH: Story sequencing

Name _____

The wind and the sun

Colour the pictures. Cut out the paragraphs.
Put them in order to tell the story.

'Now it is my turn,' said the sun
and he began to shine.
It got hotter and hotter.

The wind saw that the sun had tricked him.
He was so cross that he howled and
blew over the mountains.

1

The wind thought he was stronger than the sun.
'Very well,' said the sun.
'Let us see who is the stronger.'

'I shall be first,' said the wind and
he began to blow.
But the harder he blew the more
the man wrapped his jacket around him.

The sun saw a man walking down the road.
'The one who can make the man
take off his jacket is the stronger,' said the sun.

'This is a very hot day,' said the man
and he took off his jacket.

ESSENTIALS FOR ENGLISH: Story sequencing

Name _____

The oak tree and the fir tree

Colour the pictures. Cut out the paragraphs.
Put them in order to tell the story.

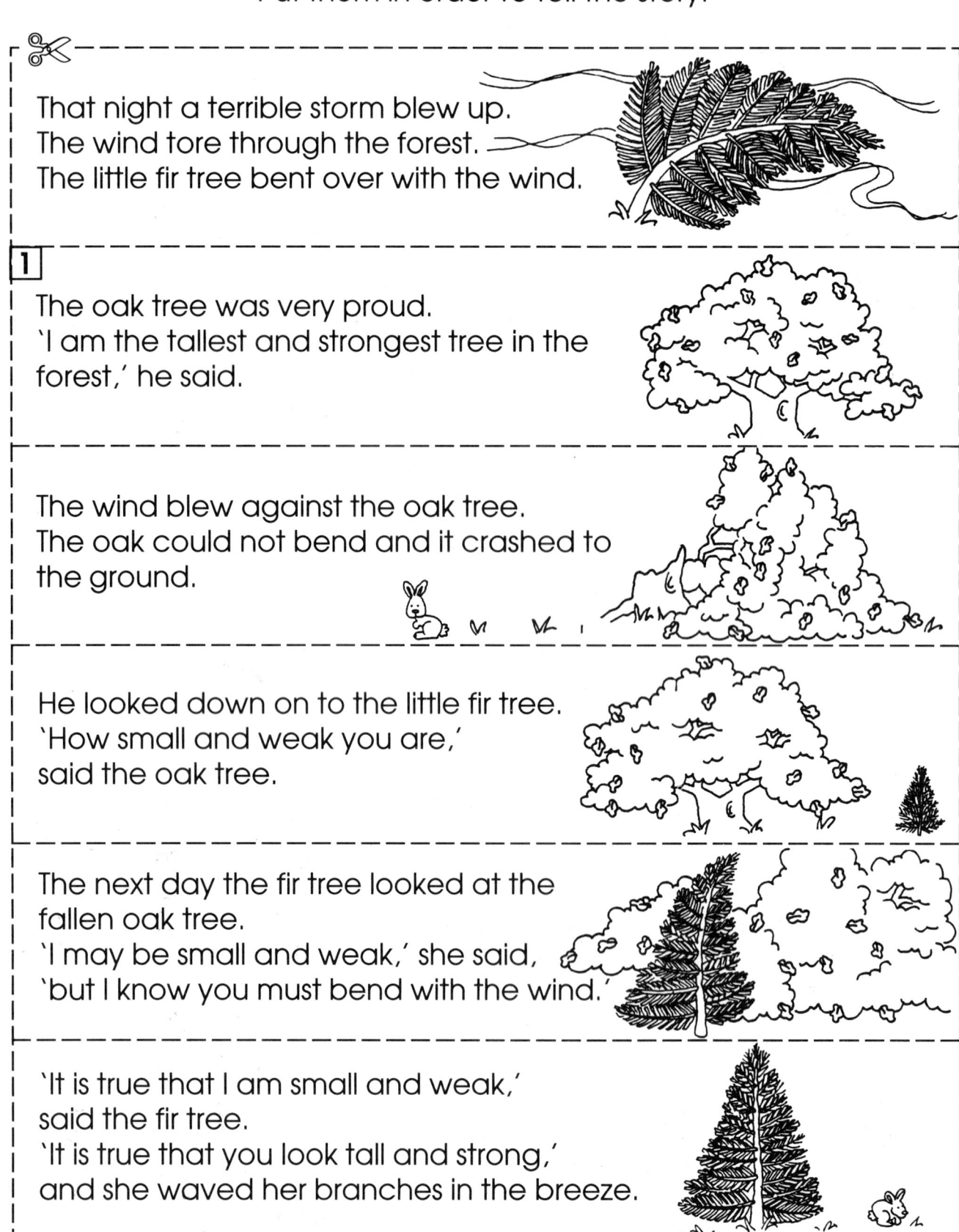

That night a terrible storm blew up.
The wind tore through the forest.
The little fir tree bent over with the wind.

1

The oak tree was very proud.
'I am the tallest and strongest tree in the forest,' he said.

The wind blew against the oak tree.
The oak could not bend and it crashed to the ground.

He looked down on to the little fir tree.
'How small and weak you are,'
said the oak tree.

The next day the fir tree looked at the fallen oak tree.
'I may be small and weak,' she said,
'but I know you must bend with the wind.'

'It is true that I am small and weak,'
said the fir tree.
'It is true that you look tall and strong,'
and she waved her branches in the breeze.

ESSENTIALS FOR ENGLISH: Story sequencing